Stewart Carswell

For Miranda,
Thank you for your support!
Hope you enjoy the book

Earthworks

Best wishes

Stewart
Carswell

Indigo Dreams Publishing

First Edition: Earthworks
First published in Great Britain in 2021 by:
Indigo Dreams Publishing
24, Forest Houses
Cookworthy Moor
Halwill
Beaworthy
Devon
EX21 5UU

www.indigodreams.co.uk

ISBN 978-1-912876-58-7

British Library Cataloguing in Publication Data. A CIP record
for this book can be obtained from the British Library.

Designed and typeset in Palatino Linotype by Indigo Dreams.
Cover design by Ronnie Goodyer at Indigo Dreams
Printed and bound in Great Britain by 4edge Ltd.

Papers used by Indigo Dreams are recyclable products made
from wood grown in sustainable forests following the guidance
of the Forest Stewardship Council.

"Marks in the ground assert the person has unquestionably been alive. He has made contact with the earth. Whatever else may be in question, this is not."

~ *Infinite Ground,* Martin MacInnes

CONTENTS

III.

Earthworks

I.

Earthworks

Sutton Hoo

What brought you here? To be raised
on the shoulders of men, to be the cargo
of flesh and riches delivered to the earth
beneath the heap of soil.

What brought you here? To ride
in a curve up the combe, to be transformed
in the barrows of the burial ground,
to sail the long night to bone and rust and rot.

What brought you here? To dig
and expose a nation's identity, to yield
to the face exhumed, to be a tourist
in summer beside the roped-off grass.

What brought you here? To return in twilight,
when no-one can tell where your dreams
may lead you. The land is an open book
and the king lies beneath every line of England.

Earthworks

Barbury Castle

I retreat up the escarpment
to within the stoop and rise of ramparts

in a ring adjacent to the Ridgeway—
the ancient route that aided travellers, easing their journey—

and the view across to the closing down factory,
the assembly line producing its last car

before closure. My last line of defence
is the history marked on the landscape

ignored for centuries. I pitch a well-executed story
from within the fort. Make something

from it. There is little time.
Go on. Make yourself.

Mast year

Fire!—thousands of shells
all toughened and strengthened,
shot from the sentinel towards the target
and fire!—another round, thousands of them,
the whole vessel stocked and loaded,
every action leading to this moment of impact
and fire!—another round, thousands of them

all dropping towards the softly rotten forest floor.
Thousands of them. It's a mast year:
when the oak is overwhelming
the forest with acorns.
Saturation, its best chance of victory,
and its legacy: a new life.

Squirrels are unprepared
for the autumn barrage.
They collect their quota,
stash it in a winter stockpile
and leave the surplus dormant.
They can't take it all away
but I can: I check the trap,
reap a fresh squirrel from the metal noose
and drop it in the sack.
I prey upon these creatures.
It's a tough season to weather
and you don't stay alive without preparation
and I mean to survive.
Or at least, for as long
as my stub of life permits me.
The house is waiting:
the thatch needs thickening,
the axe needs sharpening,
the stew needs a squirrel.

a spray of snow
             blasts the side
     and leaves
             white ripples in the bark's furrows

a sway of snowdrops
             blooms with the thaw
     and leaves
             white petals across the forest floor

an acorn cracks its shell
                and shoots
            through to light,
rising through a chorus
                of song thrush
            and wood warbler
to reach the height of the canopy collage

Each year it unfurls fresh sails
above the undercurrent of bluebells.

Each year it grew another ring,
anchored another root.

When your country knocks
you don't say no.
Saplings turn to veterans

and beyond these shores
there's opportunity for war
if you search far enough:

this one encloses the land
behind lines of fresh fencing
and now is prime for felling.

The trunk supports the crown,
the enclosure has grown
and when our country comes knocking

we'll play our part,
sharpen the saw blades
and supply the shipyard.

Hear the sawing,
hear the falling,
here the procession

away from the stump.
Six thousand unique shapes,
each ingrained with history.

get to it:
> *the hammer the axe the adze and the chisel*

quick, there is a war
> *the keel the planks the stem and the frame*

supply the timber
> *the deck the stern the hull and the mast*

serve the country
> *the root the branch the trunk and the figurehead*

shipshape

*

Two years at sea. We have pursued
to the far shore of the Atlantic and back
and forced our foe to moor in port.
The latest report from watch

is they're preparing to sail again,
to break the blockade
and march their ships in a line,
aiming their cannons at victory.

Two years at sea. We are eager
for conflict to resolve the tension.
The time draws near when we must engage
and deliver the glory we promised.

I don't know if we'll return.
I pray we do but nothing is certain or fixed
any more. Give my love to the children:
I did this for them, for their future.

God, I hope we're right. Two years at sea
and I have forgotten how sweetly your voice sings.
Tomorrow may be my last day. But it is too late
to change course and turn around.

A map of stars

Light crosses light years to reach us and the stars
appear small and dim from here. As time expands,

the names of school friends recede when the divide
widens from the years we remember them over.

So when I look back I think of my friends
as constellations and see patterns in those distant lights,

connecting together the faint memories from youth
to create a set of stories to navigate by.

Extinction on the tenant farmer's holding

"The tenant of the property, a Scotch farmer, said he had for some time
been manuring his fields with the bones of extinct animals which ages
ago ranged over his holding."
                                          ~ *The Western Mail, 7th March 1874*

The cave housed a treasure-trove of bones,
relics of creatures extinct for millennia,
the protein roasted for nutrition and flavour.

My tenant farmer had them crushed up
and ground down to spread across his rented fields,
fertilise the soil, raise crops from bone.

In the hearth-light, in the blinking dark
I have a vision: we are all
tenants to Earth. With my complicity

in the relentless way he administers
and disregards the outcome of extinction,
solely to prolong our own survival,

I fear how my own bones may be exhumed
and powdered and manured across fields
if humanity itself collapses into extinction.

The architect

The line closed and the track upon it
was lifted, scrapped, sold; the connection
cut between riverside villages.
The bridge remained: a hulk, abandoned.

No-one crossed it—there seemed no need to.
The houses faced away from the river.
Rusting, weakened, it faded

and no-one noticed it vanish. The local paper
said it collapsed in a storm
but there's a rumour going round
it was sabotaged—that's my suspicion too,
it was destroyed by the opposition

and I know it's me
they're coming for next.

Sanctuary

Lancaut

I. C13

A peninsular posturing as an island
downstream and on the opposite bank
from God's eyes in Tintern. Accessed
only via the landward hillside,
protected by screens of woodland,
Wyndcliff overlooking like a fortress.

And at the locus of the scene
stands the infirmary, or perhaps history
has shielded here a leper colony
(who can tell? who is close enough?),
the garden embedded with remedies.
Seclusion; isolation.

II. 2020

Isolation; seclusion.
Here at the border, where the saline river arcs
and farmland runs out into woodland,
Wyndcliff rises opposite like viewpoint
or lookout, its ramparts topped
with roadblocks and lockdowns.

Beside the ruined church on the English bank
of the Wye I wash my hands in the river
for 20 seconds, and kneel and offer
the only question that matters from this position:
what will it take to hold you
and to touch again across borders?

Fences

Winter brings hunger and cold
flocks across fences, and in this garden
they are lucky to have small berries to pluck.

But they will be uprooted, forced
to cross the next fence. Go
and find another patch to settle on

while we huddle and we feast
by our fireside, we rise
only to burn another log.

Locked pools

It has to be cold enough
to settle, to remain solid, fixed
and compressed together
with what lies beside it.

Yes, cold enough that the ponds
have already frozen over
and with no warmth to pass on
the ground is locked by frost.

And that is where the falling and drifting
halt and the settling begins.
The blown snow banks up
flake by flake against our door

and we have no choice
but to settle for ourselves,
and if there is still no warmth
there will be no thaw.

The fern

Metal shelves. Catalogued. Rows and rows.
Fluorescent lights. Carpet tiles.
Outside it rained and birds waited
in the branches on the edge of town.

There was one copy, odd
and out of place: the cover was firm
and earthy, something you could bank on
for good foundations; the pages
grey like lichen. I opened it
and it creaked like a ship shifting course.
Pressed flat between two pages

I found a fern, a brush of green and yellow.
Had it grown in the rich soil of the book?
Or had someone hidden it from the efficient winter?
I took it
            as a warning against trespassers.
With the fern in my pocket I saw the forest
flanked on ridges of surrounding hills
and in defiance I broached it
across the boundary defined by ferns.

*

A pulse of wind and a wave of sound
breaks through my canopy. Dead branches
snap and drop. The floor crackles
and crumbles under footsteps. By nightfall
no sight, no sense to guide you,
just lashes of ferns,
losing and lost.

St. Anthony's Well

Abenhall

Come here when your life is clogged
or blocked by boulders.
Come here despite your judgement.

Come here, where the secret water-hoard
begins to seep through filters of roots,
the whole hill weeping its catchment rainfall
through a tear in the soil at this spring.
A thin trickle, a sparkling gift

for life: one by one
descend the steps into the chill of water,
immerse your tender body. And rise again,
step upon the earth revived.

Know it is a gift.
Know it as salvation.

Sleepers

A curtain of ferns
spreads at eye height
to a child and parts
from the push of a hand

to expose
the shrinking clearing
and the treasure at its centre:
an ancient sleeper

laying like a sunken casket
and shrouded by a puzzle
of oak leaves. The specimen
ornamented with metalware:

rusted plates and bolts,
brooches carried by the dead
to the next station of life.
Close the curtains. Change the scene.

A figure stands at the end
of the platform, his face masked
by a flag. Steam
spirals around him,

a spire above rows of sleepers.
There is one line
drawn from childhood
through junctions to connections,

and the destination is close
to definition.
I feel the platform vibrate
from something about to begin.

The figure sounds his whistle.
His flag drops
and it is my face unmasked
and time to leave this dream

and I see it now. The trackbed
has lost its track and I have lost
track of time. I get up
to check my phone

but there's no signal
and my daughter is asleep,
habitually dreaming
of a better life to travel in

and I see it now.
The ancient sleeper
is a relic, an inherited burden,
second-hand history.

I step outside
and the first engine of the day
sets out light and I see it now:
I know what to do.

NB

I live in a place where I can watch
the seasons change. I mark time
by the colour of the leaves
I write on. I've seen all days end
with ink pouring between the lines,
night unfolding my notebook.

When the page is full I put down the pen
and a leaf falls onto the carpet. The floor
has been prepared by the Forest.
The words I've written were never mine.

Far into the deep Forest

I. Red Hart

Born out of this:

the great earth cracked
open deep
in the Forest,
hollowed out,
scowled out

with that initial chisel hit,
the hammer strike
into the veins
richer and deeper
and thicker than blood

beneath the crags
where yew trees reach
out their twisted roots
like the hand of a guide

this way

towards the fire
that smelts, purifies,
toughens the ground:

forge a tool,
leave your mark.

II. White Hart

No path leads here, just a narrow slit
through bracken that the Forest folds
closed behind me. This trail, like time,
can only take me one way.

I place my faith in becoming lost and discover
a fallen beech branch and a set of axe marks.
I break off part of the branch, carve a key from it
and pocket it as a gatekeeper drinks nectar.

I reach deeper into the Forest
disappearing through the undergrowth
while a sparrowhawk hunts beneath leaf-light
but there—
            nearly in the distance
I catch sight of a spirit fit for a king,
a glimpse imagined into reality.

He does not panic, nor turn away.
We are safe in our seclusion,
in the alcoves of bracken.
I know his eyes are not for seeing

but for seeing into, each one
with a great black pupil at its centre
like a mine shaft. I see the message there:
I close my eyes and I follow.

III. Black heart

Oak stands around all sides.
Squat brick ridges of buildings
beside the great dirt pyramid,
and at the heart of the complex
are two wooden towers,
not leading upward
but downward by a wire.

Men emerge from the pit head
with black dust scraped from the face.
When they leave at the end of the shift
I plant the wooden key in the soil
and enter the cage below the tower. The gate shuts,
the winding gear grinds and growls
as I descend across the threshold
of one forest into another.

The veins are thin.
I stoop and step along the passage
towards the sound of a miner
working the gale, a nelly shedding
its dull heat across his face,
a trick of light and shade.

Where do we go when they stop the pumps
and the hollow seams flood?

You must make your living somehow, old butty,
just like we've had to do here.
But find some other fuel to work from.
Follow the seams that lie under where you've been
and heave that blackness on out to the light —
only then'll you see what it's all worth, you will.

But a draught snubs out the candle
and he vanishes into darkness,
leaving me alone in someone else's past.
Unlit and enlightened
I grope back to pit bottom,
enter the cage, and ascend.

Now I must search for words
that will reach into eternity,
born from another fuel, a dark fuel
rooted out from my own narrow chambers.
Below the trees used as props
find the fuel and cast a light,
craft a line to lead the way.

II.

The wedding present

My gift for you was an acorn.
I told you to plant it
in your garden so you could always be
within reach of a forest.
So you planted it. And with time and rain
a forest grew around your house.
Fawns graze at your door,
ferns are window frames,

and you are a neighbour
to oak. Observe the seasons
and the lessons they carry.
Collect twigs and moss
and learn to build a nest:
make it hard against the wind
but soft against the skin.
Home should be a place to return to.

Learn when it is time to let go
and learn how to let go.
Leaves do not fall far,
so don't be scared to let in new light.
Gather acorns, share them with your children,
and remember how small each beginning is.

Fawns do not stay, but you will find
a set of antlers each year
outside your door. Oak is a marker
for home and marks the starting point.
Measure time in rings and anniversaries.
Always be within reach of a forest.

Crow's nest

You're picking planks
of thick twigs to build up
high up in a mast buoyed by a green sea
and assemble them
into the ragged nook of your nest.

Keep lookout safe on your high perch, peer
beyond the horizon. Something new
coming from a hatched egg.

You see what happens next?
Oh crow, tell me what happens next.

Patience

It is here too early.
Snow has smothered the garden
and the yellow star

is struggling on its green stem.
I can only watch and love
across this unwelcome cold

from beside the empty cradle,
patient,
at our home.

Together

Underneath the park bench
were four loose pieces of a jigsaw
face down in the frost. I turned each one over
and they were all sky.

Is that always the hardest part to get right?
I look up to the real thing
and with my son in my arms I can't tell
where one piece ends and the next begins.

Earthworks

West Kennett

I migrate back to this farmland
burdened for summer with corn,
where the mound distorts the harvest

and the great stones form the façade
of a house that swallows the dead
and has for centuries. On a ledge

inside the entrance a line of faces
stares down at me, their flesh
behind glossy feathers, and guarding

its nest is the swallow,
inverting the tomb into a cradle,
raising five lives from this chamber.

The calling

Stepping along the ragged lane
cooled by two hedgerows
she stopped, raised a suntanned hand
into morning air.

Did you hear that?
Was that the cuckoo?

she asked. All I'd heard
was my beating footsteps, so I paused,
and listened beyond myself. And from somewhere
near the river or closer
than expected I heard
the statement of its character.

Cuckoo
Cuckoo
Cuckoo

I turned back to her,
the air between us still as a mirror,
and her face bore a new familiarity.

Cuckoo
Cuckoo
Cuckoo

I turned to her
a second time but she had gone with the calling.
A yearning to follow
but I know

I mustn't
I mustn't
I mustn't

Earthworks

Little Doward

The ramparts have diminished in height.
Almost untraceable, almost unbelievable.
The area of the interior now vacant

as a clearing. The exterior occupied
by the Forest: where it encircles
the periphery and extends no further.

This is the defence. Trust that no-one
can enter or escape the Forest.
It is your guardian now.

From the estuary

Mud will flow upstream on high tide
and taint the clear course of the river
as it flows through the estuary.

This is the broadest river stretch
where everyone is aware of endings
but a precise end is hard to define.

When does a river have sufficient salt
to clean wounds? With which mark
did I decide that this was enough?

To the source

Everyone is aware of endings
but a start is hard to find.
Only after the flow rate has increased

do you consider that narrow stream,
long ago, how it now has developed
force and momentum and definition.

Knowing the ending, would you recognise
the source? Which drop of rain
was the trigger that set the river running?

Barn owl

I know your favourite bird is not a barn owl
because on the phone you told me
it's hard to love something when you rarely see it.

Evenings of summer meadows
empty and dim, waiting at a regular post
outside the field frame.

And now, when I wear a white shirt
on the bus ride between fields to see you,
you wait   for something to love.

Another life

I hear you're married now
and living on a hill with a daughter.
Tell me how that feels,
watching someone else becoming
the person that you wish you were.

A beach redrafted

Let's vent this rage by stoning the ocean
with the endless stockpile of pebbles
that the waves carve
out of several million years of coastline

like a poet carving words
from cliffs entrenched with history,
torturing verses out like blood
let from a stone, only for

the pebbles, the bloody words to be loosed
by the ocean upon the shoreline then dragged
back, churned in shifting waves
and structured by the poet as a beach.

In a cove, name unknown

I remember this beach differently:
I think the tide was lower last time
and it felt warmer, presumably summer.

The terns are still here.
They dive and break the surface,
make final preparations before they migrate

to the other side of the earth.
A journey as certain
as how tides follow the moon

and death follows life.
The year turns
and life turns

to ash in an urn
that we scatter
while we form

silence with the words
we can't say, the comfort
we no longer provide for each other.

A field of dew

I never polish my shoes. The scuffed fronts
are worn and show the dirt of all places I've been to.
And I know you would always follow.

This morning I rose quietly as a sunrise,
walked a field of dew to pretend wet shoes
could be clean. I return to you. I begin again.

III.

Watercourse

The brown churn of a border,
its meanders swinging like axe heads.
Rain long ago on untraceable mountains

helmet domed like a willow on the riverbank

that fell in measures
to sweep through history as a river.
These gifts

shield, ceremonial or protector

wrapped with the ribbon of water.
This is the barrier between here
and where here could've been.
I call out of another language

sword, unsharpened, snapped halfway

across the threshold of cultures,
where water eases earth

panelled cauldron
brimming with life and death and life

through muddy swirls and layers the sediment,
where the border and the limit of understanding
shifts slowly and thoroughly
over time.

Eye to eye

Start from what you know:
an eye. A gemstone in a socket.

This insight, and the tangled swirl
resolves into a skilful geometry:
a gilded arch, a hunched outline

of a staunch boar guarding a forest trail
and back-lit, with dawn light:
a glowing rim around the dark maze of bristles,

mud daubed upon the snout
and its ears erect, alert
to the sounds that shudder the forest:

a domain far from transparent museum cabinets,
beyond the reach and leer of kings.

Eddies curl   unfurl like buds
Bladderwrack sways in the current like bracken waving with the wind
                                    in a dark summer woodland
Sunken to the depth of the floor

                                                    is a wreck of oak,
    soaked and rotten,
        recognisable by shape   and strength
                        of the **timbers**
        that hold together   that branch from a spine
            upward   and lightward
                    positioned to belong in support of another
                            as though they are still
                            a part of a forest,
                    the change is only in
                        the water level

Changes

I've seen snow at dawn, fields under flood,
bluebells and green leaves and the river at dusk.
I've seen all this in the same place. All that changes

is light and colour and how we see the world.
Time brings these changes to life. We see the old forms
filled with new ideas and despite the change

we love it still. Our love adapts too but it is the same love
that holds us to each other; each time I go
it is the same love that draws me back to you.

December

I'm sorry, but each year when I put up the tree
it conceals the photo I have on the wall of you
from a war I was too young to know.

But there is the all-seeing angel—I placed it
at its vantage point six foot up
so it can be there for you through December,
to keep watch over you when I couldn't.
Everyone needs someone to...

When it's late and I'm alone with whisky
and Christmas lights I imagine you returning,
stepping out of the frame to become my angel
on the tree. This time of year
everyone needs someone to keep them company,
                    an angel to believe in.

The Wye, Belmont Woods

after Brian Hatton

All water will flow past this point
at some point. You cannot know
or follow the course beyond now,

not even your own. The sun has fallen
in the field behind the trees.
The woods thicken.

The sky fails
to a desert-vague grey.
I see my reflection

in a gun barrel. I aim
my eyes at the landscape,
draw on it to understand

Pine

We're standing outside the church door
in the clearing, me under a veil
like a ghost, you in your uniform

days before you vanished into camouflage.
Months now since I last heard news.
I pine for you. The conifer

towers surround the village
and I grow darker in their shade.
I'd die to be closer to you.

I see three soldiers at night armed
with saws, felling the pine
to make a path to the clearing.

After nights of cutting I see you
walking the wide avenue home
under moonlight. Your body

is silver, the prize for not winning.

On the anniversary

You walked the path between the pines
that led down to the water,
down to the sloping flow
of the ocean upon crushed sand
because it's where she told you to let go
so it's where you've come to let go.

A cove of ash, boulders
ground into grains on the shore—
too many to count, but for a moment
it is you two alone by the water.

You make a vow to return each year
but an echo
is not an exact repetition,
and when you walk the path again
the journey will take you further
each year that you repeat it.

Silver turn

Littledean

A trace of a temple, an outline
of a religion emerging
through the scraped-back layers
of brushed earth. A square courtyard
stone-walled and fountain-fed.
An alcove for a nymph.

In the latest trench, dark soil
gives way to buried metal
glinting at the edge of the Forest:
a silver torc, a thousand years untouched,
an almost-loop like a thumb and a finger
of a god holding on around your wrist.

Here it is, the twisting silver
River Severn flat on the dark vale plain
below the hilltop temple. That same torc
magnified across open ground, broad
when the current's surging strong,
or a delicate line at low tide.

If I wear this meander around my home
I know my home is safe and guarded
on the land under the eye of a spirit,
shielded by the arc of water
at turns gold and silver
at turns of Earth and tide.

Outlines

I see your outline on the beach
coiled in stone. You were here

when the ground was soft. You fell asleep
and the world formed around you.

We live our best and reminisce;
others remember where we rest.

*

The dead have a homing instinct
like no other. They return
                         to the ground
they were raised on, last the rest of time
at peace in one place.
                    My children
get closer each year. I know my parents
through their headstones.
                         They came together,
eventually, and now stone lets them go
nowhere. I reach out
                   for them,
touch cold letters.

*

I never learnt to love
until it was too late
to know how late it was.
So: love now.
Love completely.

The future won't care:
love cannot be preserved
like an outline can.
Love is malleable;
death is firm.

*

What remains of us is left
in stone of our homeland. Marked
with an outline or initials, a trace
of the dates. Every headstone is a reminder

that stone cannot judge who should be preserved.
We live our best, create an impression,
and then it's chance. From my own grave
I lose control over how I will be remembered,

how my craft will be requisitioned
or reformed from the pieces I leave behind.
I can entrust nothing more to fate. Rest.
I will not go when you look away.

At a crossroads in the Forest

Look through the window
and see the place you are standing:
at a crossroads in the Forest.

Alone. The conifers
that buttress you into cloister silence
are unanswerable as ancestors.

Take whichever path you want:
they all loop back to here.

Devil's Chapel

Bream

A metal gate rusted and bent
out of shape. No longer neat
and secure, even though
good fences are still needed.

The track beyond is narrow, faint,
like a vein seen under skin.
Yew trees wedge their roots
into limestone stacks

and crack a fracture slowly open.
False pits plunge in black crevices
and red rocks are clamped
green with moss. A cleft

barely a foot wide is blocked
by dead black logs and ivy
hanging from holly trees, and it narrows
to a slit in the vein of stone

then blooms into a cavern
that extends beyond reach of torchlight,
that extends to the dark limits
where imagination takes over.

Cut right and out pores the core.
Scratched with charcoal
onto the wall of the red chamber
is the stark outline of a stag

injured in the neck, the wretched beast
preserved in torment for art.
My pen, sharp as a blade,
runs out on the last line.

Listen to this

The river is fed by brooks that pour
sound down the hillside. A season of rain
fattens it. The level has risen
higher than I expected, but it is level still

and *that* is important: to stay balanced
no matter how much rain
has fallen, no matter how much you want
to flow with that water away from this place.

Earthworks

Offa's Dyke, Tidenham Chase

Requisition soil.
Scoop it from a ditch,

raise it and turn the earth
against your enemies.

A narrow rampart
to mark the frontier of tolerance.

Divide land by language.
Make a border out of nothing.

*

Forget the origin. Forget the cause
and let borders be overrun

by bluebells. Let ramparts
degrade. Let the yew tree

entrench its thousand-year-old ambition
beneath the needless ditch and dyke.

Let a man walk the earth
and know that this is the last earth.

NOTES

Mast year: a year in which a tree produces a high number of seeds. A mast year is usually followed by several years of low seed production.

Extinction on the tenant farmer's holding: the epigraph is from a newspaper article titled "The Bone Caves of the Wye", detailing the discovery of prehistoric animal bones in a cave system on the banks of the River Wye near Symond's Yat (West), Herefordshire.

Eye to eye: the poem is a response to the Sutton Hoo shoulder clasp in the British Museum.

The Wye, Belmont Woods: the title is from a painting by Brian Hatton.

ACKNOWLEDGEMENTS

Acknowledgements are due to the editors of the following where some of these poems first appeared: Algebra of Owls, Elsewhere, Envoi, Ink Sweat & Tears, Reach Poetry, Sarasvati, The Fenland Reed, The Lighthouse, and Under the Radar; and to the editors of the following anthologies: Anthology Eighty Four (Verve Poetry Press, 2019), and In Other Words (Allographic, 2016).

With grateful thanks to Martin MacInnes for permission to use the epigraph.

Some of the poems here were previously published in the pamphlet *Knots and branches* (Eyewear Publishing, 2016).

Thank you to Sarah Mnatzaganian and all at the Ely Stanza Group, whose insightful comments helped shape early versions of many of these poems.

Thank you to the poetry community in Cambridge and the Fens for their support; in particular to Fay Roberts, Beth Hartley, and Elaine Ewart, whose work in organising and promoting spoken word events has given me the invaluable opportunity to develop as a writer and performer.

And thank you to Rebecca, for Wednesdays.

Indigo Dreams Publishing Ltd
24, Forest Houses
Cookworthy Moor
Halwill
Beaworthy
Devon
EX21 5UU
www.indigodreams.co.uk